The Best We Can Be

Inspired by Angela Y. Nixon
Illustrated by Chandra Gunawan

JG| JENIS GROUP, LLC

The Best We Can Be Copyright © 2017

Any unauthurized reproduction, use, coping, distribution or sale of these materials — including words and illusrations — without written consent of the author is stricly prohibited. Federal law provides severe penalties for unauthorized reproduction, use, copying or distribution of copyrighted material.

Book cover design by Angela Y. Nixon
ISBN 978-1942674191
First Edition: November 2017

For bulk order prices or any other queries, please contact aynixon@jenisgroup.com

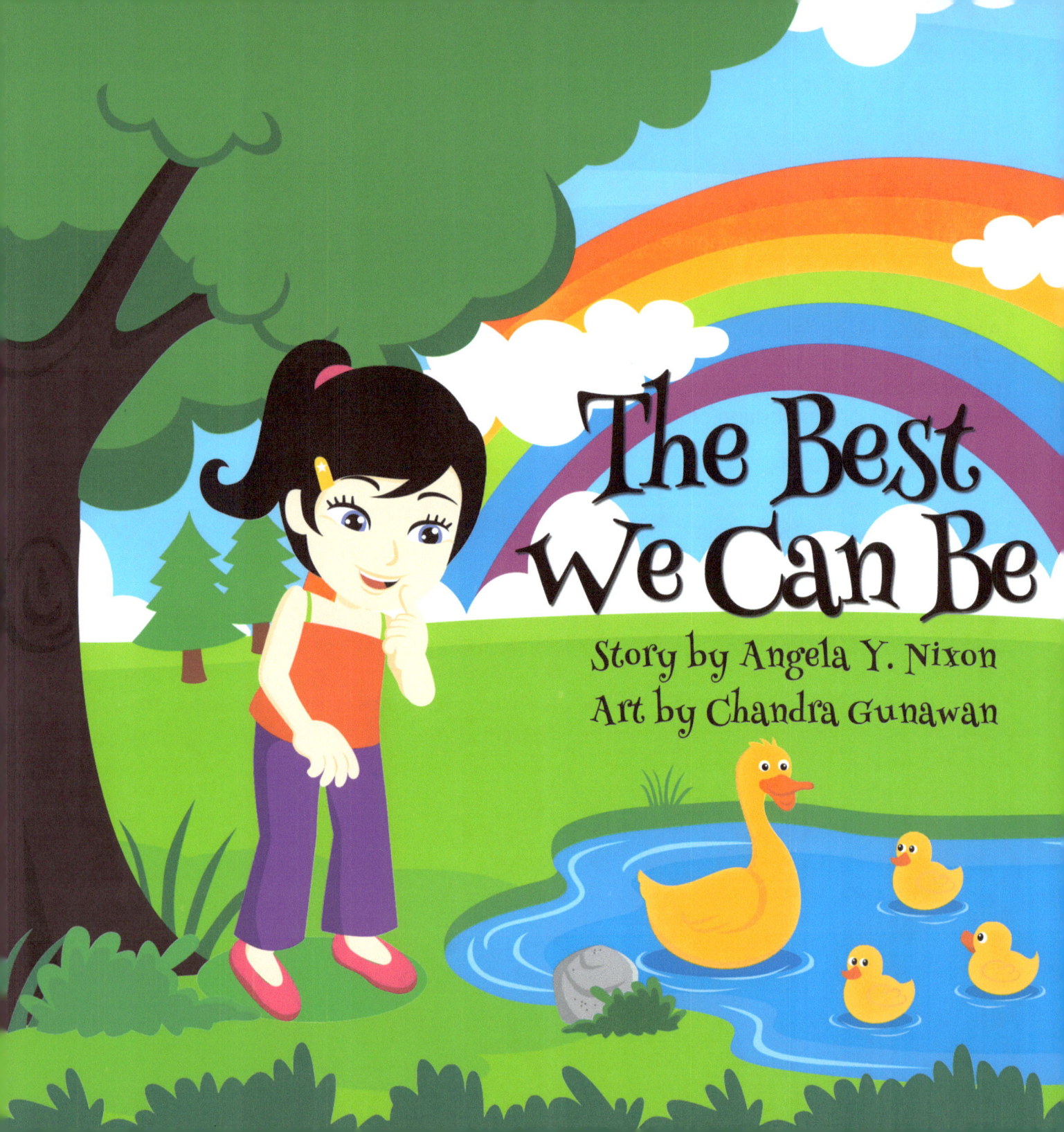

This book belongs to

_____

Hey, girls, do you have a minute?
I've got a story to tell — and you are in it!
It starts at the beginning with "once upon a time,"
and the "happily ever after" is yours and mine!
You see, there is only one "you," and one "me."
But together, we're unstoppable, wouldn't you agree?
So stand up tall, be strong and bold.
You are a beautiful sight to behold!

Do you know what an amazing girl you are

This story continues with girls of all ages,
sizes and colors, talents and stages.
Girls who enjoy each and every day,
hanging out at the beach or swimming in the bay.
The world is ours to search and explore.
Adventures await from shore to shore!

What great adventure would you like to go on someday?

When we stick together, through thick and thin,
There is only one outcome, and that is to win!
We are sisters, neighbors, and trusted friends
who live life together until the end.
So, let's give a thumbs-up and a pat on the back,
after all, we have made a pact,
to be honest and fair, faithful pals
who build each other up — we are those kinds of gals.

Do you need a thumbs — up today?

Oh, the many talents we have to share,
like painting or dancing, there's no need to compare.
We cheer each other on, we are on the same team.
There is no competition that comes between.
Girl, you are creative! You're an artist at heart!
Whatever you put our mind to, you are capable and smart.

Do you believe that?

We will dream together about what we'll become —
a doctor, a vet, even the President — which one?
Each of our stories
will take different paths,
as we make different
choices and use what we have
to make a difference
in this big, wide world.
You are amazing! Don't forget that, girl!

What amazing thing would you like to do one day?

You might even become a star,
and let the whole world know just who you are!
Sing it loud and sing it clear.
Don't be afraid of anything, do you hear?
I'll be in the front row, clapping the loudest,
cheering for my friend, I'll be the proudest.

Do you ever dream of becoming a star?

Close friends have fun just hanging out.
A good friend like you, I wouldn't do without.
By spending time together, we learn many things,
like our favorite colors, or if we like green beans.
We can have a picnic or play tag outside,
take a walk around the block or go on a bike ride.

Do you know what a good friend you are?

You will be there for me and I will be there for you,
a shoulder to cry on when we are feeling blue.
We will be helpers to everyone around,
climb trees to get kittens safe to the ground.
We will set an example for our younger friends
by teaching them and lending a hand.
This will make others smile, and you smile too.
Because helping people is being the very best you!

What makes you happy?

Together, we are unstoppable! Together we can stand.
That is how this great story ends.
Remember, there is only one "you" and one "me."
Bold, and strong, and the best we can be!

The End

About the Author
Angela Nixon aspires to do God's will for her life.
She is a wife and mother of four children.

Angela is a God-fearing
and God-loving woman who
loves people and she aspires to inspire
others through the gifts
and talents God has given her.

Do you have a desire to write and need direction?
Please contact Angela Y. Nixon
aynixon@jenisgroup.com